ld growth forests

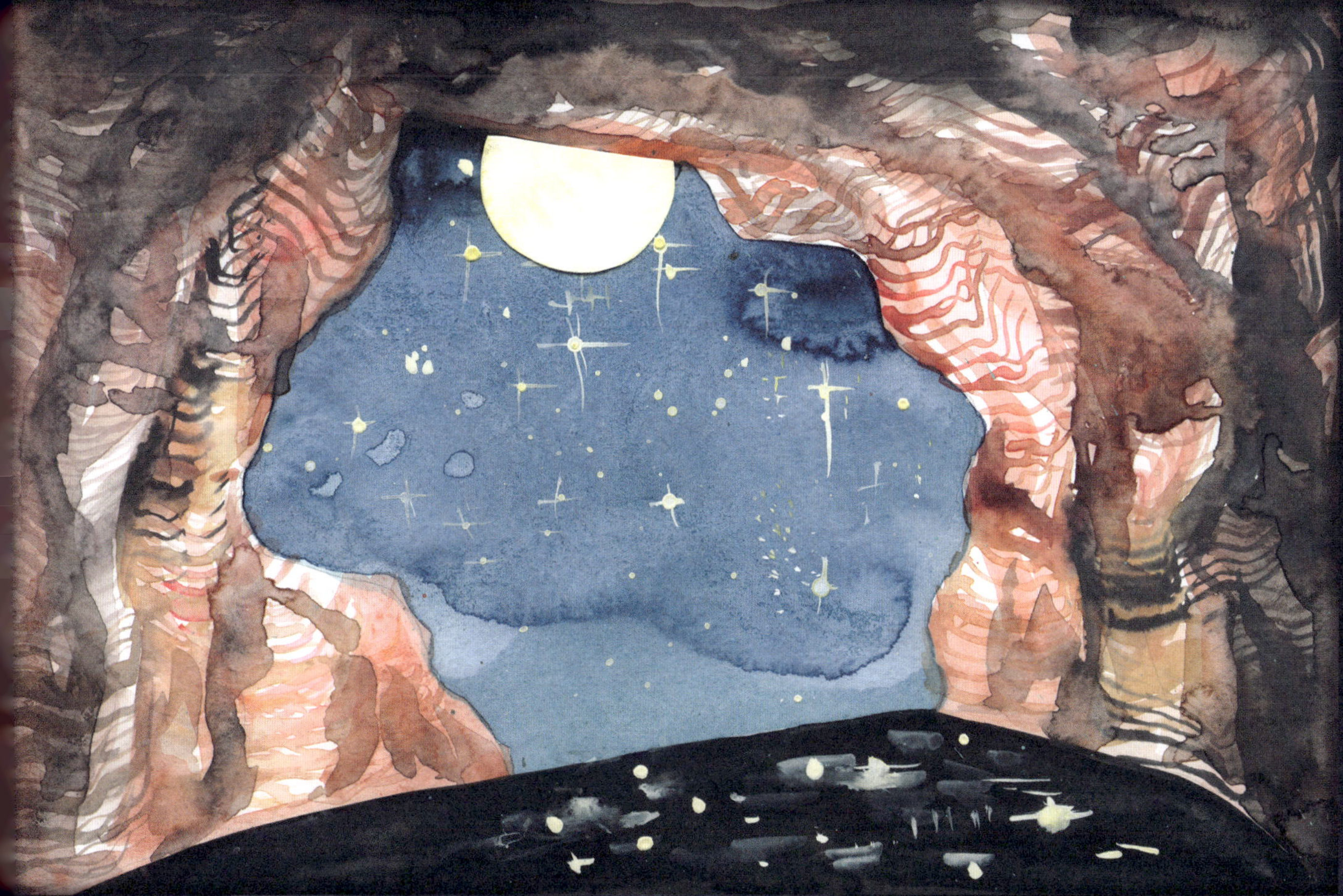

Caves

To my amazing circle of friends and
fellow night owls who love to sleep
well into the day and come alive when
the moon is high in the sky.

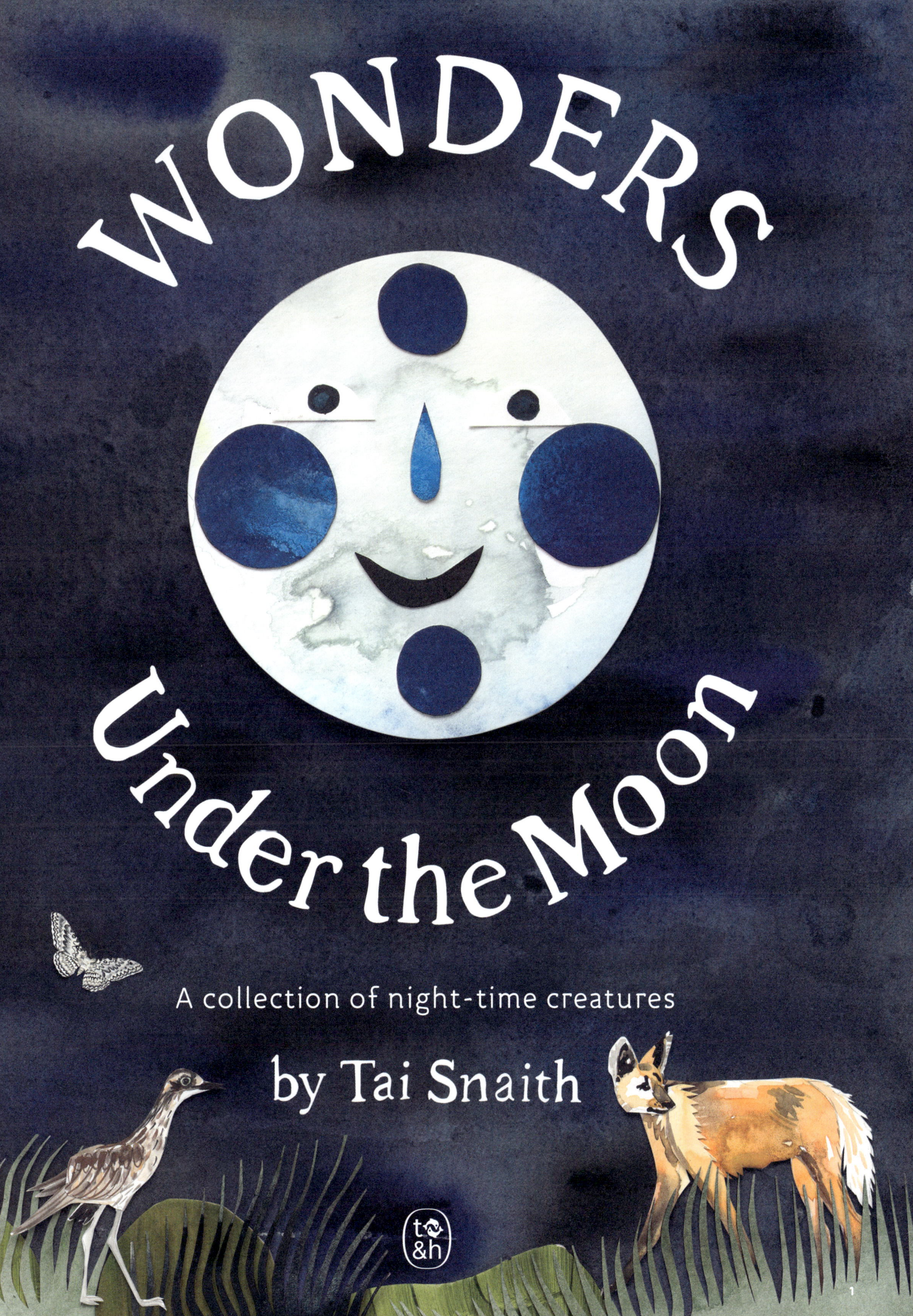
WONDERS
Under the Moon
A collection of night-time creatures
by Tai Snaith
t&h

Who you'll find inside

Introduction

As an artist I find nocturnal creatures very inspiring for so many reasons. Many of them have huge eyes or ears so they can see and hear in the dark, which makes them so cute and fun to draw! But it's not just how they look – they often have mad skills! Many of them are silent and stealthy and have incredible night-time vision. They also often have super cool details and features, such as glow worms and fireflies that can glow in the dark using bioluminescence, or bats who use echolocation to navigate and find food. Some have incredible survival mechanisms, like the pangolins and hedgehogs who can roll into a protective ball when they are threatened by a predator. Some are just beautiful, like the incredible moths and owls with their patterns and intricately detailed feathers. I'm in awe and love drawing their awesomeness.

This book is a selection of my most beloved nocturnal creatures and a kind of artist's reference book for you to use. I want to share these creatures with you to bring attention to their wonderous features and hopefully inspire you as well. In this book you will find page after page of weird and wonderful nocturnal creatures who come to life as the Moon rises each night. Just like the daytime or diurnal (meaning active during the day) creatures in my last book *Wonders Under the Sun*, these nocturnal animals share this planet with us; we just don't see as much of them as they just come out and play when we go to bed!

Within this book I have grouped the animals into slightly unusual collections. Unlike the usual scientific groupings, here you will find animals put together because of how they behave (loners, tricksters and noisy party animals) as well as how they look. Similar to animals active during the day, you will find nocturnal creatures in a wide range of habitats such as moist and humid forests and even your front or back lawn. From the tiniest bugs and bats to the regal lions and tigers, these creatures all play important roles in Earth's survival and ours.

Sadly many of these special night-time legends are in serious trouble. Next to some of the animals' names in the book, you might notice an icon. This means these animals are vulnerable, endangered or critically endangered. One of the main reasons these animals are threatened or endangered is because they

are losing their homes, or habitats. At the start and end of the book, I have illustrated a range of the habitats in which these wondrous creatures live. Places like forests and wetlands are especially important as they have such rich biodiversity, with many species of plants and animals living together. As humans, we must help protect these habitats and regenerate damaged habitats or create new ones where we can.

Next time you go outside at night ask yourself, 'Who else is out here that I can't see?' These hidden night creatures are just as important to our natural world as the ones we can see during the daylight hours. Use your ears and other senses to give you hints.

There is a list near the end of this book with some ideas for things you can do in your own home or community to help protect your local wildlife and provide more places for plants and animals to live. You might also like to grab a headtorch and an adult and go for your own discovery walk at night, making a list of who you can see hiding in the dark. Let's pay them some attention and help them in any way we can!

Each night is alive with so many curious creatures. Instead of just going to bed to dream at night, let's put our heads together, join our dreams and work hard to imagine a better future for these creatures, where they can live and thrive in peace as we sleep.

Key

V Vulnerable E Endangered C Critically endangered

Fantastic Features

We have big eyes or big ears

18 cm

9 cm

0 cm

1. Merriam's kangaroo rat

2. Grey mouse lemur

3. Horsfield's or western tarsier V

4. Thick-tailed gecko

5. Philippine tarsier

6. Senegal bushbaby

7. Mohol bushbaby

8. Great potoo

9. Red slender loris E

10. Bengal slow loris E

11. Andean or Peruvian night monkey E

Great potoos are masters of camouflage. They often perch motionless on branches with their eyes closed and look exactly like part of the branch.

0 cm
25 cm
50 cm
12. Desert long-eared bat
13. Brown long-eared bat
14. Spotted bat
The spotted bat has ears over half as long as the rest of its body! A group of bats is called a colony.
16. Ghost bat V
17. Big-eared woolly bat
15. California leaf-nosed bat
19. Spinifex hopping mouse
20. Greater glider V
Greater gliders can glide for 100 metres and can change direction mid-flight. They steer with their long tails.
18. Long-eared jerboa
21. Snowshoe hare
22. Fennec fox
23. Greater bilby V
24. Bat-eared fox
25. Caracal
26. European hare

Sonic Superheroes

We use echolocation to navigate

Aye-ayes use echolocation to find their food. Using their middle finger, they tap on logs and, depending on the sound their finger makes on the wood, they will know if there are grubs hiding inside.

Echolocation is when animals use sounds to figure out where objects are. Bats make high-pitched sounds (that we can't hear) that bounce off surfaces to let them know how close they are. This helps to stop them from crashing into things.

Prickly Personalities

We are spiky and spiny

12 cm

6 cm

0 cm

44. Jewel spider

45. Cairo spiny mouse

46. Long-eared hedgehog

47. Western European hedgehog

48. Lesser hedgehog tenrec

Although lesser hedgehog tenrecs looks similar to hedgehogs, they aren't actually related! In fact, tenrecs are more closely related to elephants as they are both part of a group of animals originating in Africa called Afrotheria.

49. Four-toed hedgehog

50. Stump-tailed porcupine
51. Asiatic brush-tailed porcupine
52. Mexican hairy dwarf porcupine
53. Canadian porcupine
54. Indian crested porcupine
55. African crested porcupine
0 cm
25 cm
50 cm

Lively Loners

We prefer to forage alone

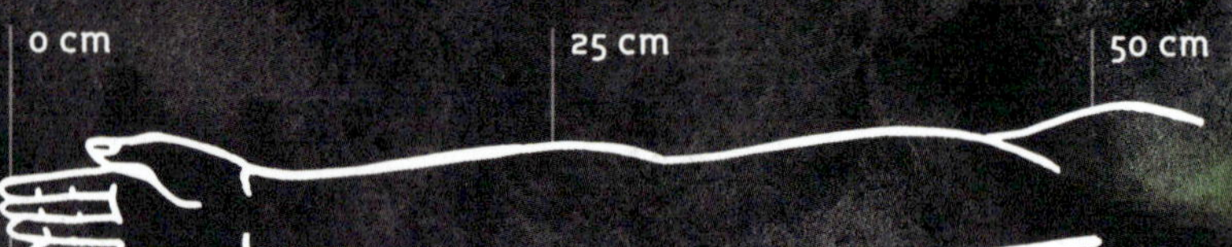

56. Mexican mouse opossum

57. Bush rat

58. Ermine

59. Yellow-crowned brush-tailed rat

60. Javan ferret-badger

61. Eastern barred bandicoot V

62. Asian palm civet

63. Crab-eating or South American raccoon

Did you know tamanduas have a sticky tongue up to 40 centimetres long? That's almost as long as 3 pencils! This makes them really good at catching bugs and reaching into the narrow tunnels of termite mounds and ant colonies.

Aardvarks are colourblind but can see well in the dark, so they can eat up to 50,000 ants a night! Aardvarks are usually found alone, but a group of aardvarks is called an armoury.

Slimeballs and Slippery Characters

We have no hair and we don't care!

Velvet worms squirt sticky slime from their heads to ambush their prey. The slime then hardens and traps the prey so the velvet worm can take a bite and slurp up its insides.

Even though they look like a lizard, marbled salamanders are actually amphibians. They have really thin skin that is always moist, similar to frogs.

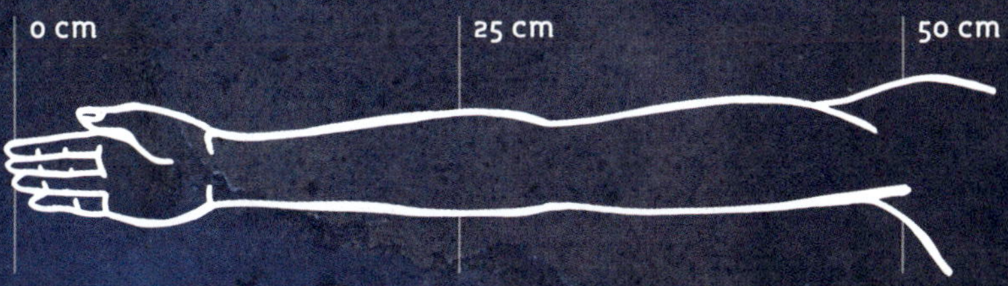

80. Carpathian blue slug

82. Leopard slug

83. Cane toad

81. Night snake

85. Eyelash viper

Eyelash vipers not only have very long eyelashes, they have very long fangs too. Their bite can be extremely painful and deadly.

84. Desert rosy boa

86. Milk snake

87. Brazilian rainbow boa

88. Philippine cobra

Terrific Tails

We have long, fancy extra bits

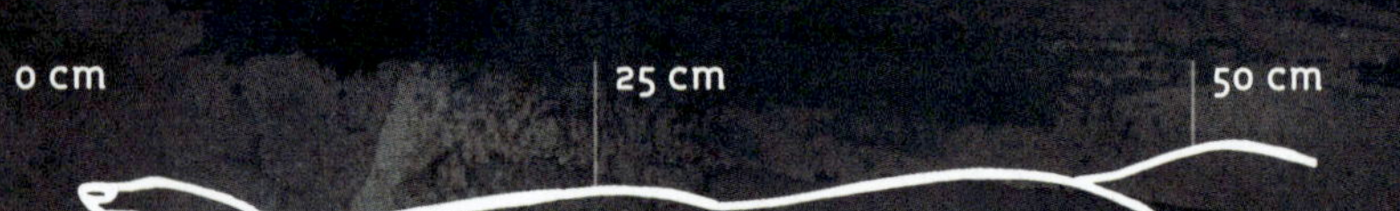

89. Fat-tailed dunnart

Fat-tailed dunnarts eat as much as they can when there is lots of food available. They then store this extra body fat in their tails for when there isn't as much food around. This is how they get their name!

90. Spectacled dormouse

91. Chinchilla

92. Luzon bushy-tailed cloud rat E

93. Striped possum

94. Hooded skunk

95. Striped hog-nosed skunk

96. Ringtail

97. Cacomistle
98. Nine-banded armadillo
99. Red panda E
130 cm
65 cm
0 cm
Did you know that nine-banded armadillos can dive underwater, hold their breath for up to 6 minutes and walk along the bottom of rivers? A group of armadillos is called a roll.
100. Northern or Guadeloupe raccoon
101. Raccoon dog
102. Striped skunk
103. Binturong V
104. Red fox
105. White-tailed deer
106. Maned wolf

Party Animals

We're a noisy, social bunch

107. European mole cricket

108. Olive-green coastal katydid

When a katydid wants to make a sound, it rubs its wings together. This makes a loud, high-pitched noise that they hear through ears on their front legs.

12 cm

6 cm

0 cm

109. Striped marsh frog

The most surprising thing about the little grasshopper mouse is its high-pitched howling, which may be a way of scaring off predators as well as communicating with other grasshopper mice.

111. Northern mockingbird

110. Northern grasshopper mouse

112. Night parrot C

113. Whip-poor-will

The bush stone-curlew uses its high-pitched screech-like call to contact mates and family members in the dark of night. Nicknamed the 'screaming woman bird', their blood-curdling calls are often mistaken for a human in trouble.

Biters and Bloodsuckers

We like the taste of blood

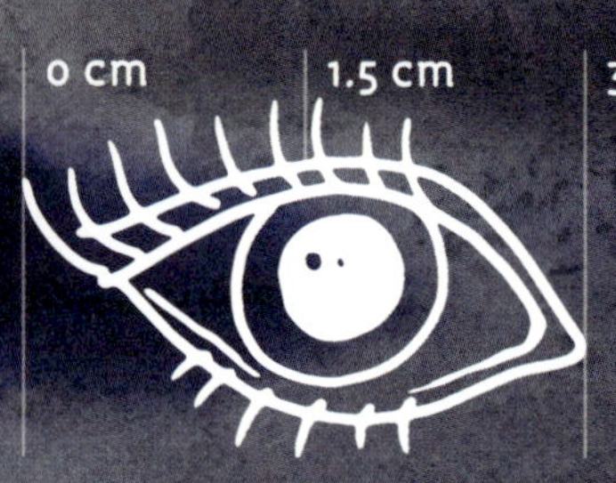

123. Common bed bug

124. Indian red scorpion

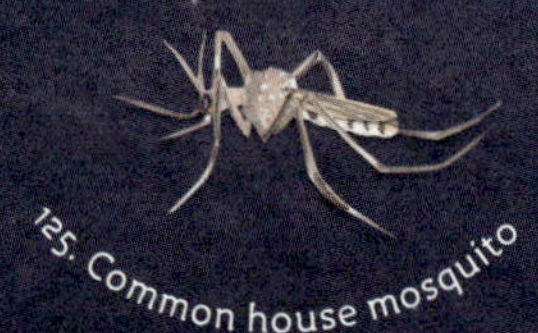

125. Common house mosquito

126. Tiger leech

Tiger leeches feed on blood. A leech will attach itself to its prey and drop off when it's full.

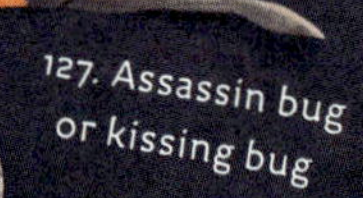

127. Assassin bug or kissing bug

128. Hairy-legged vampire bat

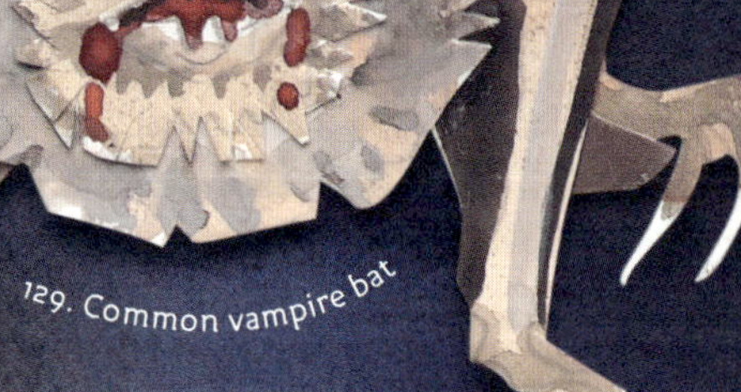

129. Common vampire bat

130. White-winged vampire bat

12 cm

6 cm

0 cm

131. Red claw scorpion

132. North American medicinal leech

133. Giant desert hairy scorpion

134. Giant blue scorpion or Asian forest scorpion

135. Amazon giant leech

136. Gila monster

Gila monsters can eat a lot. In just one meal adults can eat over one-third of their body weight, while baby monsters can devour half of their body weight. That's the same as a nine-year-old kid eating 15 kilograms of pasta for dinner!

Nimble Night-time Ninjas

We are the acrobats and aerialists of the animal world

The critically endangered mountain pygmy possum weighs as little as 40 paper clips. It has a long, strong tail that it uses as an extra limb, wrapping it tightly around branches as it climbs.

Known as the rarest mammal in North America, black-footed ferrets are very playful, especially as babies. They like to wrestle and perform a 'ferret dance' where they leap and jump backwards. A group of ferrets is called a business or busyness.

Pangolins are elusive, mysterious creatures with very little known about them. What we do know is that when they are in danger, pangolins roll into an almost perfect ball, exposing their armour of scales to protect themselves from predators.

Radiant Radicals

We glow up and get down

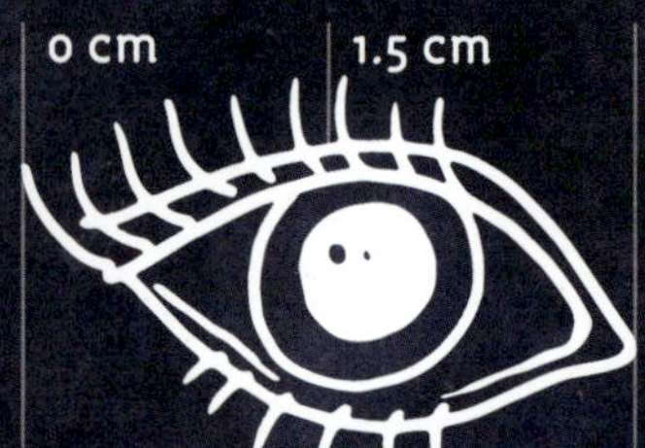

152. Lightning bug or synchronous firefly

Male lightning bugs or synchronous fireflies flash to impress female fireflies. The males all flash in unison, and stop in unison, while flying! A group of fireflies is called a sparkle.

154. Eastern firefly

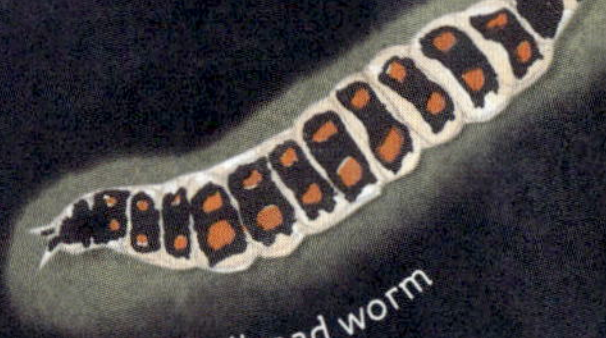
155. Railroad worm

158. Glowing click beetle

159. Centipede

160. Headlight click beetle

163. Namib sand gecko

153. New Zealand glow-worm

Glowing worms and beetles are bioluminescent, which means their bodies can make light.

157. Western banded glow-worm

156. Common European glow-worm

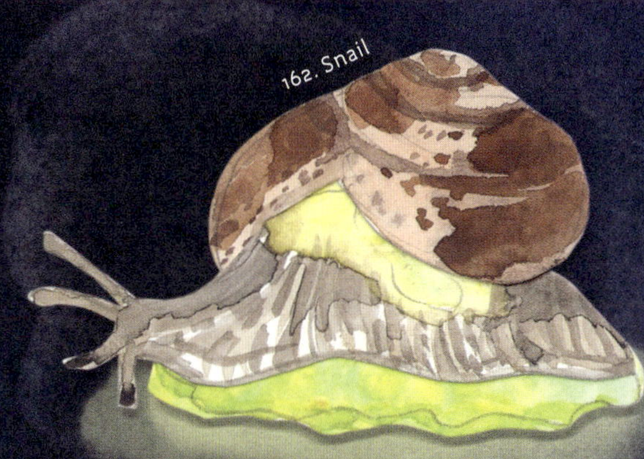
162. Snail

161. Sequoia millipede

You won't see the Cranwell's horned frog glowing at night-time, but other frogs might see its glow. Scientists recently discovered that the frog appears fluorescent green under blue light. They believe it might be only visible to other frogs as a way to signal to one another.

164. Cranwell's horned frog

Bright Eyes

We are attracted to the bright lights

The tentatively named Venezuelan poodle moth is not officially classified as a species as yet. It was discovered and photographed by one person in 2009 in Venezuela and identified as a member of the *Artace* moth genus.

167. Cinnabar moth

166. Vine sphinx moth

168. Muslin moth

172. White plume moth

173. Elephant hawkmoth

Shaped like an aeroplane and designed for speed, sphinx moths can travel at over 48 kilometres per hour. That's faster than an Olympic gold medallist sprinter!

176. Giant leopard moth

177. Luna moth

180. Lime hawkmoth

Did you know that moths don't have noses? They use their antennae to sense the smells in their environment and guide them towards food or mates. A group of moths is called an eclipse.

182. White witch moth

Pouncers and Purrers

Watch out, we may be behind you!

Clouded leopards are very acrobatic. They live mainly in trees and can swing from branches, jumping up to 4.5 metres from branch to branch. That's like jumping over 2 table tennis tables! A group of leopards is called a leap.

185. Black-footed cat V
186. Margay
187. Flat-headed cat E
130 cm
65 cm
0 cm
190. Bobcat
191. Canadian lynx
196. Cougar or mountain lion
195. Asian golden cat
198. Tiger C

Haunting Hooters

We like to hang out and hunt at night

199. Elf owl

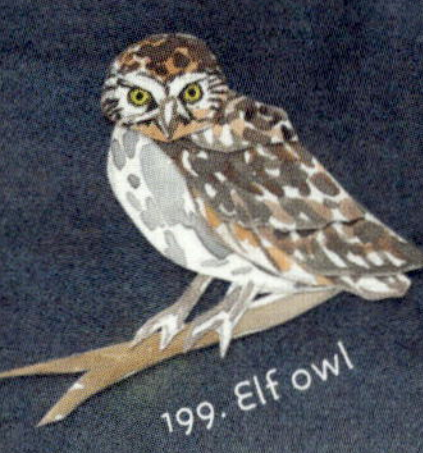

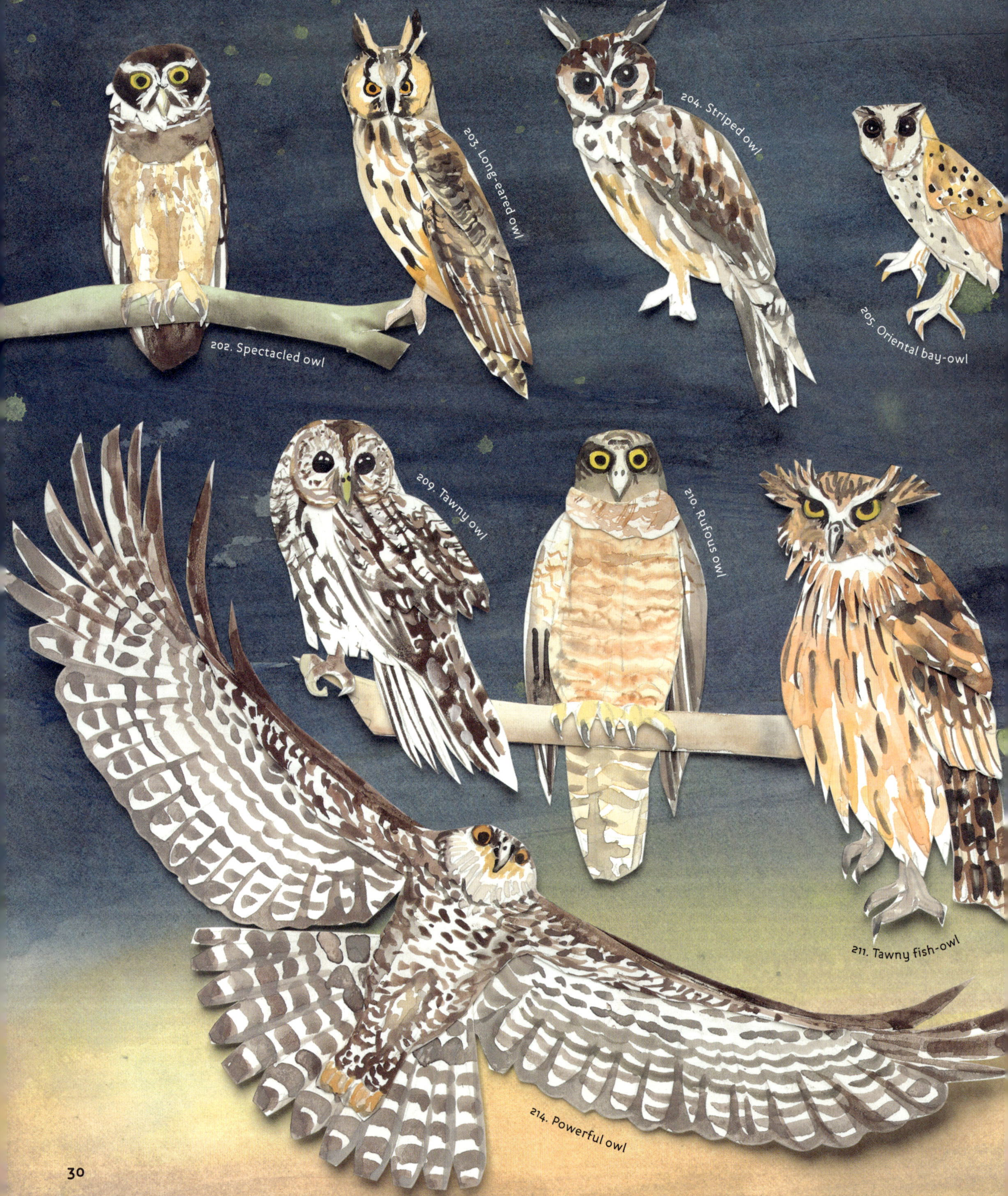
202. Spectacled owl
203. Long-eared owl
204. Striped owl
205. Oriental bay-owl
209. Tawny owl
210. Rufous owl
211. Tawny fish-owl
214. Powerful owl

Great grey owls are one of the biggest owls in the world! They have incredibly good hearing thanks to their curved dish-like faces that work like a funnel to amplify the sounds of their prey. A group of owls is called a parliament.

Ways we can help

1. One way to help protect native wildlife is to keep your pet cats and dogs inside at night. An easy way to tell if it's ok for them to go outside is if you can see the sun.

2. Animals need darkness and quiet at night to hunt, breed, navigate, communicate and sleep. Light pollution can kill or harm animals by disrupting their behaviour and destroying food sources. If you're outside at night, try to keep quiet and don't use a super bright light.

3. Try not to ever use mouse or rat poison. If owls eat the dead rats or mice, the poison kills them too! If your parents do need to use poison, suggest researching first-generation poisons, which are less dangerous.

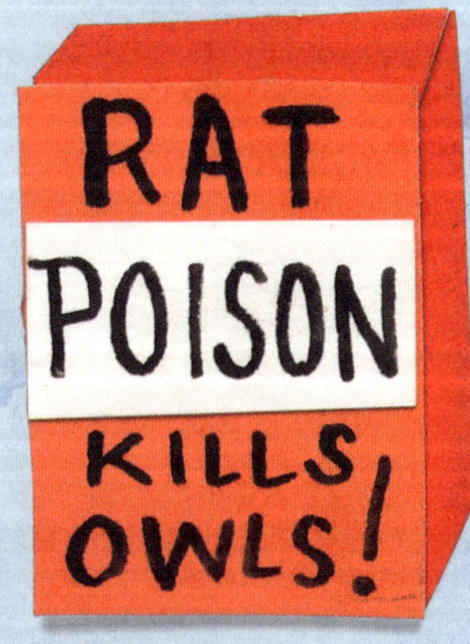

4. Owls, gliders and lots of other night animals need hollows to nest in. Trees do not create hollows until they are at least 50 years old, so it is important that we leave trees to get old and even keep dead trees for animal habitats. Unfortunately, many of these old trees are being unnecessarily logged as we speak. One way to help protect these old trees from being cut down is to show that you care and that you are not happy about animal habitats being turned into woodchips. You could make a sign and ask your parents to take you to a protest or write an email to your local member of parliament expressing how important it is that these trees are protected.

5. If you need to net your fruit trees, use netting with small holes (less than 5 millimetres) so bats, birds, snakes and mammals won't get tangled.

6. Fill your birdbath at night too. Lots of nocturnal animals like bats and owls will appreciate a fresh drink, especially on hot summer nights.

7. If you ever find an injured or abandoned nocturnal animal such as a possum, bat or bird, use a towel to gently catch them. Put them on a woollen or fleece blanket in a box with airholes in a quiet, dark place. If it's a cold night, fill a plastic bottle with hot water from the tap (not boiling), wrap it in a tea towel, and put it under the blanket. Contact your local wildlife carer, vet or ranger for advice on what to do next. Vets don't usually charge for treating injured wildlife.

8. It is just as important to plant flowering trees and plants that are native to your local area for nocturnal animals as well as birds and bees during the daytime. Flowers provide animals like bats and possums with important sources of food in the form of nectar and pollen.

Creature details

Fantastic Features

1. **Merriam's kangaroo rat** | *Dipodomys merriami* | Mammal | Found in arid regions of south-western USA and Mexico
2. **Grey mouse lemur** | *Microcebus murinus* | Mammal | Found in dry forests of western Madagascar
3. **Horsfield's or western tarsier** | *Cephalopachus bancanus* | Mammal | Found in forests in Borneo, Indonesia and Malaysia | V
4. **Thick-tailed gecko** | *Underwoodisaurus milii* | Reptile | Found across a wide variety of habitats in southern Australia
5. **Philippine tarsier** | *Carlito syrichta* | Mammal | Found in rainforest of the Mindanao region of the south-eastern Philippines
6. **Senegal bushbaby** | *Galago senegalensis* | Mammal | Found in forests and bush of sub-Saharan Africa
7. **Mohol bushbaby** | *Galago moholi* | Mammal | Found in semi-arid and savanna woodland and gallery forests in southern Africa
8. **Great Potoo** | *Nyctibius grandis* | Bird | Found in forests and rainforest in Central America
9. **Red slender loris** | *Loris tardigradus tardigradus* | Mammal | Found in wet lowland forests of south-western Sri Lanka | E
10. **Bengal slow loris** | *Nycticebus bengalensis* | Mammal | Found in tropical, subtropical and semi-evergreen rainforest in South-East Asia and India | E
11. **Andean or Peruvian night monkey** | *Aotus miconax* | Mammal | Found in humid cloud-forest of the Andes Mountains, Peru | E
12. **Desert long-eared bat** | *Otonycteris hemprichii* | Mammal | Found in arid habitats of North Africa, sub-Saharan Africa, West and Central Asia, the Middle East, India and Pakistan
13. **Brown long-eared bat** | *Plecotus auritus* | Mammal | Found in temperate forests, woodland and parks in Europe and Asia
14. **Spotted bat** | *Euderma maculatum* | Mammal | Found in forests, deserts and caves across North America
15. **California leaf-nosed bat** | *Macrotus californicus* | Mammal | Found in caves and abandoned mines in the deserts of south-western USA, Mexico and Central America
16. **Ghost bat** | *Macroderma gigas* | Mammal | Found in forests, savanna, shrubland, mountains and caves across northern Australia | V
17. **Big-eared woolly bat** | *Chrotopterus auritus* | Mammal | Found near fresh water in tropical rainforest and cloud-forest throughout Central America and northern South America
18. **Long-eared jerboa** | *Euchoreutes naso* | Mammal | Found in shrubland and deserts across Mongolia and China

19. **Spinifex hopping mouse** | *Notomys alexis* | Mammal | Found mostly in deserts and grassland in Central and Western Australia
20. **Greater glider** | *Petauroides volans* | Marsupial mammal | Found in eucalyptus forests in eastern Australia | V
21. **Snowshoe hare** | *Lepus americanus* | Mammal | Found in tundra, forests, agricultural areas and wetlands throughout northern America
22. **Fennec fox** | *Vulpes zerda* | Mammal | Found in northern Africa and the Sahara Desert
23. **Greater bilby** | *Macrotis lagotis* | Marsupial mammal | Found in deserts and grassland in Western Australia, Northern Territory and far western Queensland, Australia | V
24. **Bat-eared fox** | *Otocyon megalotis* | Mammal | Found in grassland and savanna in eastern and south-western Africa
25. **Caracal** | *Caracal caracal* | Mammal | Found in a variety of habitats throughout Africa, Central Asia and south-western Asia
26. **European hare** | *Lepus europaeus* | Mammal | Found in agricultural areas, shrubland and grassland throughout Europe; introduced to the Americas, Australia and New Zealand

Sonic Superheroes

27. **Great fruit-eating bat** | *Artibeus lituratus* | Mammal | Found in forest canopies, caves and buildings from Mexico to northern South America
28. **Honduran white bat** | *Ectophylla alba* | Mammal | Found in tropical rainforest of western Central America
29. **Northern short-tailed shrew** | *Blarina brevicauda* | Mammal | Found in forests, shrubland and wetlands in Canada and northern USA
30. **Common or Eurasian shrew** | *Sorex araneus* | Mammal | Found in cool damp forests, woodland and grassland from the UK to Russia
31. **Dobson's shrew tenrec** | *Microgale dobsoni* | Mammal | Found in humid forests and agricultural land of eastern Madagascar
32. **Mexican long-tongued bat** | *Choeronycteris mexicana* | Mammal | Found in desert scrub, forest canyons and caves in southern North America and Central America
33. **Brazilian free-tailed bat** | *Tadarida brasiliensis* | Mammal | Found in caves and buildings throughout southern North America and parts of South America
34. **Woodland dormouse** | *Graphiurus murinus* | Mammal | Found in forests, savanna, shrubland, grassland and wetlands from Ethiopia to South Africa
35. **Peter's dwarf epauletted fruit bat** | *Micropteropus pusillus* | Mammal | Found in forests, savanna, shrubland and grassland in western, south-western and central Africa
36. **Eastern red bat** | *Lasiurus borealis* | Mammal | Found in temperate and tropical forests across eastern USA and warmer areas in winter

37. **Pied butterfly bat** | *Niumbaha superba previously Glauconycteris* | Mammal | Found in tropical lowland moist forests of Ghana, Cote d'Ivoire and Democratic Republic of the Congo
38. **Canyon bat** | *Parastrellus hesperus* | Mammal | Found in forests, grassland, deserts, cliffs and buildings in southern North America

39. **Aye-aye** | *Daubentonia madagascariensis* | Mammal | Found in rainforest, forests and plantations mainly in eastern Madagascar | E
40. **Oilbird** | *Steatornis caripensis* | Bird | Found in tropical rainforest at night and mountain caves or ravines during the day in north-western South America
41. **Hammer-headed bat** | *Hypsignathus monstrosus* | Mammal | Found in forests, swamps and mangroves of central Africa
42. **Hoary bat** | *Lasiurus cinereus* | Mammal | Found in forests, woodland, caves and urban trees throughout North and South America
43. **Spectacled flying fox** | *Pteropus conspicillatus* | Mammal | Found in tropical rainforest of north-eastern Australia and Papua New Guinea | E

Prickly Personalities

44. **Jewel spider** | *Austracantha minax* | Arachnid | Found in woodland and gardens in Australia

45. **Cairo spiny mouse** | *Acomys cahirinus* | Mammal | Found in arid rocky regions in northern Africa

46. **Long-eared hedgehog** | *Hemiechinus auritus* | Mammal | Found in arid shrubland, deserts and steppes from Egypt to Mongolia

47. **Western European hedgehog** | *Erinaceus europaeus* | Mammal | Found in temperate woodland, grassland and near human settlements across Europe and Central Asia

48. **Lesser hedgehog tenrec** | *Echinops telfairi* | Mammal | Found in forests, shrubland and savanna of south-western Madagascar

49. **Four-toed hedgehog** | *Atelerix albiventris* | Mammal | Found in deserts in central and eastern Africa

50. **Stump-tailed porcupine** | *Coendou rufescens* | Mammal | Found in the dry mountain forests in north-western South America

51. **Asiatic brush-tailed porcupine** | *Atherurus macrourus* | Mammal | Found in cultivated areas, forests and rainforest across South-East Asia

52. **Mexican hairy dwarf porcupine** | *Coendou mexicanus* | Mammal | Found in forests from Mexico to Panama

53. **Canadian porcupine** | *Erethizon dorsatum* | Mammal | Found in a variety of habitats such as tundra, forests, grassland and desert shrubland from North America to northern Mexico

54. **Indian crested porcupine** | *Hystrix indica* | Mammal | Found in a variety of habitats such as rocky hillsides, scrubland, grassland and forests throughout south-eastern and Central Asia and parts of the Middle East

55. **African crested porcupine** | *Hystrix cristata* | Mammal | Found in a variety of habitats such as forests, savanna and rocky areas in Italy, the Mediterranean coast of Africa and a narrow band across central Africa

Lively Loners

56. **Mexican mouse opossum** | *Marmosa mexicana* | Marsupial mammal | Found in forests, woodland and mangroves from eastern Mexico to Central America

57. **Bush rat** | *Rattus fuscipes* | Mammal | Found in forests, woodland and heath in southern and eastern Australia and southern Western Australia

58. **Ermine** | *Mustela erminea* | Mammal | Found in forests, woodland, wetlands and open areas across Europe, Greenland, North America and Asia

59. **Yellow-crowned brush-tailed rat** | *Isothrix bistriata* | Mammal | Found in lowland forests and river floodplains of the western Amazon Basin including Peru, Bolivia, Venezuela, Colombia and Brazil

60. **Javan ferret-badger** | *Melogale orientalis* | Mammal | Found in forests in Java and Bali in Indonesia

61. **Eastern barred bandicoot** | *Perameles gunnii* | Marsupial mammal | Found in grassland and grassy woodland in Tasmania and reintroduced to two Australian islands | V

62. **Asian palm civet** | *Paradoxurus hermaphroditus* | Mammal | Found in temperate or tropical forests and developed areas across Asia

63. **Crab-eating or South American raccoon** | *Procyon cancrivorus* | Mammal | Found in a variety of habitats such as forests and land near water in southern Central America and northern South America east of the Andes

64. **Tasmanian devil** | *Sarcophilus harrisii* | Marsupial mammal | Found in forests, shrubland, heathland, grassland and caves throughout Tasmania | E

65. **Island fox** | *Urocyon littoralis* | Mammal | Found in the six largest Channel Islands off southern California

66. **American badger** | *Taxidea taxus* | Mammal | Found in dry open grassland and pastures across North America

67. **Southern tamandua** | *Tamandua tetradactyla* | Mammal | Found in wet and dry forests, savanna and shrubland in northern South America east of the Andes

68. **Fisher** | *Pekania pennanti previously Martes pennanti* | Mammal | Found in forests throughout northern North America

69. **Southern hairy-nosed wombat** | *Lasiorhinus latifrons* | Marsupial mammal | Found in semi-arid and arid grassland and woodland in southern Australia

70. **Aardvark** | *Orycteropus afer* | Mammal | Found in forests, shrubland, grassland and savanna throughout sub-Saharan Africa

71. **Snow leopard** | *Panthera uncia previously Uncia uncia* | Mammal | Found in high mountain ranges of Central Asia | V

72. **Common wombat** | *Vombatus ursinus* | Marsupial mammal | Found in temperate areas suitable for burrowing, from forests to coastal scrub and heathland in eastern Australia and Tasmania

Slimeballs and Slippery Characters

73. **Blue velvet worm** | *Peripatoides novaezealandiae* | Onychophora | Found in forests, scrub and gardens throughout New Zealand

74. **Burgundy snail** | *Attenborougharion rubicundus previously Helicarion rubicundus* | Gastropod | Found in wet forests on the Tasman and Forestier peninsulas in Tasmania | V

75. **Semi-slug** | *Helicarion nigra* | Gastropod | Found in forests and woodland throughout south-eastern Australia

76. **Red-eyed tree frog** | *Agalychnis callidryas* | Amphibian | Found near fresh water in tropical rainforest across Mexico, Central America and northern South America

77. **Giant velvet worm** | *Tasmanipatus barretti* | Onychophora | Found in wet or dry forests in north-western Tasmania

78. **Red triangle slug** | *Triboniophorus graeffei* | Gastropod | Found in forests, woodland, heathland and urban areas throughout eastern Australia

79. **Marbled salamander** | *Ambystoma opacum* | Amphibian | Found in woodland throughout eastern USA

80. **Carpathian blue slug** | *Bielzia coerulans* | Gastropod | Found in forests across the Carpathian Mountains of Eastern Europe

81. **Night snake** | *Hypsiglena torquata* | Reptile | Found in a variety of habitats throughout North America

82. **Leopard slug** | *Limax maximus* | Gastropod | Found in urban areas throughout Australia

83. **Cane toad** | *Rhinella marina* | Amphibian | Found in a variety of habitats near fresh water in southern USA, Central and northern South America, widely introduced to islands including Australia

84. **Desert rosy boa** | *Lichanura trivirgata* | Reptile | Found in a variety of habitats throughout south-western USA and north-western Mexico

85. **Eyelash viper** | *Bothriechis schlegelii* | Reptile | Found in tropical rainforest, woodland and shrubland in Central America and north-eastern South America

86. **Milk snake** | *Lampropeltis triangulum* | Reptile | Found in a variety of habitats but mainly forests in North America

87. **Brazilian rainbow boa** | *Epicrates cenchria* | Reptile | Found in forests and savanna in the Amazon Basin and eastern Brazil

88. **Philippine cobra** | *Naja philippinensis* | Reptile | Found in a wide variety of habitats in the Philippines, such as agricultural areas and forests

Terrific Tails

89. **Fat-tailed dunnart** | *Sminthopsis crassicaudata* | Marsupial mammal | Found across southern Australia

90. **Spectacled dormouse** | *Graphiurus ocularis* | Mammal | Found in rocky habitats and shrubland throughout South Africa
91. **Chinchilla** | *Chinchilla lanigera* | Mammal | Found in the mountains of northern Chile
92. **Luzon bushy-tailed cloud rat** | *Crateromys schadenbergi* | Mammal | Found in forests on Luzon Island, Philippines | E
93. **Striped possum** | *Dactylopsila trivirgata* | Marsupial mammal | Found in tropical rainforest and woodland of far north-eastern Australia and New Guinea
94. **Hooded skunk** | *Mephitis macroura* | Mammal | Found in a variety of habitats such as forests, shrubland, grassland, rocky areas and desert from southern USA to Mexico and Central America
95. **Striped hog-nosed skunk** | *Conepatus semistriatus* | Mammal | Found in forests, woodland and grassland in Mexico, Central America, north-eastern South America and eastern Brazil
96. **Ringtail** | *Bassariscus astutus* | Mammal | Found in a variety of habitats throughout southern North America, such as rocky areas, forests, shrubland and grassland
97. **Cacomistle** | *Bassariscus sumichrasti* | Mammal | Found in tropical woodland and mountain forests from southern Mexico to western Panama
98. **Nine-banded armadillo** | *Dasypus novemcinctus* | Mammal | Found in a variety of habitats such as forest, savanna, shrubland and grassland across southern North America through Central America to northern South America
99. **Red panda** | *Ailurus fulgens* | Mammal | Found in temperate forests in the Himalayan mountains across Burma, Nepal, India and into China | E
100. **Northern or Guadeloupe raccoon** | *Procyon lotor* | Mammal | Found in a variety of habitats near water throughout North America, northern South America and parts of Asia and Europe
101. **Raccoon dog** | *Nyctereutes procyonoides* | Mammal | Found in subarctic to sub-tropical forests near water across Siberia, northern China, North Vietnam, Korea, Japan and introduced to Europe
102. **Striped skunk** | *Mephitis mephitis* | Mammal | Found in forests, savanna, shrubland, grassland, farmland and suburbia across North America
103. **Binturong** | *Arctictis binturong* | Mammal | Found in tropical forests in South-East Asia | V
104. **Red fox** | *Vulpes vulpes* | Mammal | Found in a variety of habitats across the Northern Hemisphere, mainland Australia and the Falkland Islands
105. **White-tailed deer** | *Odocoileus virginianus* | Mammal | Found in a variety of habitats in North and Central America
106. **Maned wolf** | *Chrysocyon brachyurus* | Mammal | Found in forests, savanna, shrubland, grassland and wetlands in central and eastern South America

Party Animals

107. **European mole cricket** | *Gryllotalpa gryllotalpa* | Insect | Found in damp habitats across Europe and eastern USA
108. **Olive-green coastal katydid** | *Austrosalomona falcata* | Insect | Found in woodland, urban and agricultural areas in eastern Australia
109. **Striped marsh frog** | *Limnodynastes peronii* | Amphibian | Found in freshwater areas throughout eastern Australia
110. **Northern grasshopper mouse** | *Onychomys leucogaster* | Mammal | Found in shrubland, grassland and desert in North America and north-eastern Mexico
111. **Northern mockingbird** | *Mimus polyglottos* | Bird | Found in open areas and edges of forests and shrubland throughout North America
112. **Night parrot** | *Pezoporus occidentalis* | Bird | Found in shrubland and grassland in pockets in northern arid Western Australia and south-western Queensland, Australia | C
113. **Whip-poor-will** | *Antrostomus vociferus* | Bird | Found in eastern forests of North America, Mexico and Central America
114. **Little spotted kiwi** | *Apteryx owenii* | Bird | Found in forests and shrubland of Kapiti Island, other New Zealand islands and mainland sanctuaries | V
115. **Grey-headed flying fox** | *Pteropus poliocephalus* | Mammal | Found in a variety of habitats in eastern Australia such as rainforest, forests, woodland and suburbs | V

116. **Tawny frogmouth** | *Podargus strigoides* | Bird | Found in a variety of habitats throughout Australia, including suburbs
117. **Bush stone-curlew** | *Burhinus grallarius* | Bird | Found in open forests, woodland, shrubland, grassland and suburbs throughout Australia, especially in the north
118. **Golden jackal** | *Canis aureus* | Mammal | Found in open grassland and steppes from Africa to Europe, the Middle East, Central Asia and South-East Asia
119. **Kākāpō owl parrot** | *Strigops habroptila* | Bird | Found on three New Zealand islands | C
120. **Colombian night monkey** | *Aotus lemurinus* | Mammal | Found in forest on the western edge of Colombia and Ecuador | V
121. **Wild boar** | *Sus scrofa* | Mammal | Found in a variety of habitats such as forests, savanna, shrubland, grassland and wetlands throughout every continent except Antarctica
122. **Alexander Archipelago wolf** | *Canis lupus ligoni* | Mammal | Found in dense forests in south-eastern Alaska and islands of the Alexander Archipelago | E

Biters and Bloodsuckers

123. **Common bed bug** | *Cimex lectularius* | Insect | Found in beds all over the world

124. **Indian red scorpion** | *Hottentotta tamulus* | Arachnid | Found in tropical and subtropical habitats in India, Pakistan, Nepal and Sri Lanka
125. **Common house mosquito** | *Culex pipiens* | Insect | Found in a variety of temperate habitats in Europe, Asia, Africa, Australia, North and South America
126. **Tiger leech** | *Richardsonianus australis* | Clitellata | Found in fresh water throughout eastern Australia
127. **Assassin bug or kissing bug** | *Triatoma gerstaeckeri* | Insect | Found in a variety of habitats throughout south-eastern North America
128. **Hairy-legged vampire bat** | *Diphylla ecaudata* | Mammal | Found in tropical and subtropical forests, caves and arid areas from Mexico to South America
129. **Common vampire bat** | *Desmodus rotundus* | Mammal | Found in humid or arid habitats, caves and rocky areas from Mexico to South America
130. **White-winged vampire bat** | *Diaemus youngi* | Mammal | Found in tropical and dry forests from Mexico to South America
131. **Red claw scorpion** | *Pandinus cavimanus* | Arachnid | Found in savanna in Tanzania

132. **North American medicinal leech** | *Macrobdella mimicus* | Clitellata | Found in swamps throughout North America

133. **Giant desert hairy scorpion** | *Hadrurus arizonensis* | Arachnid | Found in deserts of south-western USA

134. **Giant blue scorpion or Asian forest scorpion** | *Heterometrus spinifer* | Arachnid | Found in forests throughout South-East Asia

135. **Amazon giant leech** | *Haementeria ghilianii* | Clitellata | Found in the Amazon River Basin

136. **Gila monster** | *Heloderma suspectum* | Reptile | Found in arid areas throughout southern North America

Nimble Night-time Ninjas

137. **Mountain pygmy possum** | *Burramys parvus* | Marsupial mammal | Found in the alpine regions of Victoria and New South Wales, Australia | C

138. **Feathertail glider** | *Acrobates pygmaeus* | Marsupial mammal | Found in a range of habitats throughout eastern Australia

139. **Japanese dwarf flying squirrel** | *Pteromys momonga* | Mammal | Found in evergreen forests throughout Honshu, Shikoku and Kyushu islands, Japan

140. **Sugar glider** | *Petaurus breviceps* | Marsupial mammal | Found in forests from New Guinea to northern and eastern Australia

141. **Silky anteater** | *Cyclopes didactylus* | Mammal | Found in tropical forests from southern Mexico to northern South America

142. **Common ringtail possum** | *Pseudocheirus peregrinus* | Marsupial mammal | Found in forests, savanna and parks along eastern and southern Australia including Tasmania

143. **Yellow-bellied glider** | *Petaurus australis* | Marsupial mammal | Found in eucalypt forests in eastern Queensland and New South Wales, Australia

144. **Great eared-nightjar** | *Lyncornis macrotis* | Bird | Found in forests, shrubland and grassland throughout South-East Asia and south-eastern India

145. **Sunda flying lemur** | *Galeopterus variegatus* | Mammal | Found in the treetops of tropical rainforest throughout South-East Asia

146. **Black-footed ferret** | *Mustela nigripes* | Mammal | Found in shrubland and grassland in central North America

147. **Chinese pangolin** | *Manis pentadactyla* | Mammal | Found in forests, shrubland and grassland throughout Nepal, Assam, eastern Himalayas, Burma and China | C

148. **Indian pangolin** | *Manis crassicaudata* | Mammal | Found in deserts and subtropical forests, shrubland and grassland throughout southern Asia | E

149. **Kinkajou** | *Potos flavus* | Mammal | Found in forests from Mexico to Brazil

150. **Philippine pangolin** | *Manis culionensis* | Mammal| Found in forests, grassland and agricultural areas on four western Philippine islands | C

151. **Giant pangolin** | *Smutsia gigantea* | Mammal | Found in forests and savanna throughout western and central Africa | E

Radiant Radicals

152. **Lightning bug or synchronous firefly** | *Photinus carolinus* | Insect | Found near streams in forests of the Appalachian Mountains, USA

153. **New Zealand glow-worm** | *Arachnocampa luminosa* | Insect | Found in forests, near streams and in caves across New Zealand

154. **Eastern firefly** | *Photinus pyralis* | Insect | Found near streams in meadows and woodland east of the Rocky Mountains, USA

155. **Railroad worm** | *Phrixothrix hirtus* | Insect | Found in South America

156. **Common European glow-worm** | *Lampyris noctiluca* | Insect | Found in open grassland and hedges in Europe and the UK

157. **Western banded glow-worm** | *Zarhipis integripennis* | Insect | Found in south-western North America and the Pacific coast

158. **Glowing click beetle** | *Deilelater physoderus* | Insect | Found in woodland and grassland in southern North America

159. **Centipede** | *Geophilus carpophagus* | Arthropod | Found in woodland in the UK and Europe

160. **Headlight click beetle** | *Pyrophorus noctilucus* | Insect | Found in forests throughout North, Central and South America

161. **Sequoia millipede** | *Motyxia sequoia* | Insect | Found in forests in California, USA

162. **Snail** | *Quantula striata* | Gastropod | Found in a variety of habitats across Singapore, Malaysia, Cambodia, the Philippines, Fiji and some Indonesian islands

163. **Namib sand gecko** | *Pachydactylus rangei* | Reptile | Found in arid areas of coastal Angola, Namibia and South Africa

164. **Cranwell's horned frog** | *Ceratophrys cranwelli* | Insect | Found in grassland and wetlands in Argentina, Uruguay and southern Brazil

Bright Eyes

165. **Venezuelan poodle moth** | *Artace* | Insect | Found in the Canaima National Park in Venezuela

166. **Vine sphinx moth** | *Eumorpha vitis* | Insect | Found in tropical and subtropical lowland in south-eastern North America and Central America

167. **Cinnabar moth** | *Tyria jacobaeae* | Insect | Found in grassland in Europe, Asia and North America

168. **Muslin moth** | *Diaphora mendica* | Insect | Found in Europe and temperate Asia

169. **Garden tiger moth** | *Arctia caja* | Insect | Found in forests and gardens throughout North America, Europe and Asia

170. **Southern flannel moth** | *Megalopyge opercularis* | Insect | Found in forests throughout southern North America and Central America

171. **Chinese moon moth** | *Actias dubernardi* | Insect | Found in the mountains of China

172. **White plume moth** | *Pterophorus pentadactyla* | Insect | Found in grassland, uncultivated ground and gardens across Europe, the Middle East and North Africa

173. **Elephant hawkmoth** | *Deilephila elpenor* | Insect | Found in woodland, grassland and gardens in central Europe and the UK

174. **Rosy maple moth** | *Dryocampa rubicunda* | Insect | Found in forests in eastern North America

175. **Australian bogong moth** | *Agrotis infusa* | Insect | Found in forests, woodland and urban areas across south-eastern Australia, southern Western Australia, Queensland and Norfolk Island | E

176. **Giant leopard moth** | *Hypercompe scribonia* | Insect | Found in forests across south-eastern North America and Central America

177. **Luna moth** | *Actias luna* | Insect | Found in forests of eastern North America

178. **Regal moth** | *Citheronia regalis* | Insect | Found in forests across eastern USA

179. **Oleander hawkmoth** | *Daphnis nerii* | Insect | Found in forests and urban areas across Africa, Asia and southern Europe

180. **Lime hawkmoth** | *Mimas tiliae* | Insect | Found in woodland and urban areas of Europe

181. **Atlas moth** | *Attacus atlas* | Insect | Found in tropical rainforest throughout South-East Asia

182. **White witch moth** | *Thysania agrippina* | Insect | Found in rainforest of South and Central America

Pouncers and Purrers

183. **Sand cat** | *Felis margarita* | Mammal | Found in deserts in northern Africa, the Arabian Peninsula and Central Asia

184. **Serval** | *Leptailurus serval* | Mammal | Found in forests, savanna, grassland and wetlands throughout southern and central Africa and the Atlas Mountains, north-western Africa

185. **Black-footed cat** | *Felis nigripes* | Mammal | Found in savanna, grassland and deserts of southern Africa | V

186. **Margay** | *Leopardus wiedii* | Mammal | Found in tropical forests from Mexico to northern South America

187. **Flat-headed cat** | *Prionailurus planiceps* | Mammal | Found in tropical forests and wetlands in the southern Malay Peninsula, Sumatra and Borneo | E

188. **Pallas' cat** | *Otocolobus or Felis manul* | Mammal | Found in shrubland, grassland, steppes and semi-arid regions of Central Asia

189. **African wildcat** | *Felis silvestris lybica* | Mammal | Found in most habitats except tropical rainforests in Africa, the Middle East and Central Asia

190. **Bobcat** | *Lynx rufus* | Mammal | Found throughout North America to southern Mexico

191. **Canadian lynx** | *Lynx canadensis* | Mammal | Found in forests, shrubland and grassland in northern North America

192. **Clouded leopard** | *Neofelis nebulosa* | Mammal | Found in tropical forests and shrubland from south of the Himalayas to Malaysia | V

193. **Ocelot** | *Leopardus pardalis* | Mammal | Found in forests, shrubland and savanna from Mexico to South America

194. **European wildcat** | *Felis silvestris* | Mammal | Found in various habitats throughout Europe such as forests, shrubland, grassland, wetlands and rocky areas

195. **Asian golden cat** | *Catopuma temminckii* | Mammal | Found in forests scattered throughout South-East Asia and China

196. **Cougar or mountain lion** | *Puma concolor* | Mammal | Found in forests, savanna, shrubland, grassland and desert from North to South America

197. **African lion** | *Panthera leo* | Mammal | Found in forests, shrubland, savanna and grassland across most of sub-Saharan Africa | V

198. **Tiger** | *Panthera tigris* | Mammal | Found in a variety of habitats scattered across Asia | C

Haunting Hooters

199. **Elf owl** | *Micrathene whitneyi* | Bird | Found in deserts, woodland and urban areas of southern North America

200. **Little owl** | *Athene noctua* | Bird | Found in a variety of habitats from Europe to Asia and from northern Africa to the Middle East

201. **Príncipe scops owl** | *Otus bikegila* | Bird | Found in rainforest on Principe Island off the coast of Africa

202. **Spectacled owl** | *Pulsatrix perspicillata* | Bird | Found near water in rainforests and woodland throughout Central and South America

203. **Long-eared owl** | *Asio otus* | Bird | Found in grassland and shrubland throughout North America, Europe, Asia, north Africa and nearby islands

204. **Striped owl** | *Asio clamator* | Bird | Found mainly in grassland and savanna throughout Central and South America

205. **Oriental bay-owl** | *Phodilus badius* | Bird | Found in a variety of habitats such as forests and mangroves throughout South-East Asia

206. **Barn owl** | *Tyto alba* | Bird | Found in a wide variety of habitats on every continent except Antarctica

207. **Sooty owl** | *Tyto tenebricosa* | Bird | Found in rainforest across eastern Australia and Papua New Guinea

208. **Southern boobook** | *Ninox boobook* | Bird | Found in woodland, farmland and urban areas throughout Australia and nearby islands

209. **Tawny owl** | *Strix aluco* | Bird | Found in forests, agricultural and urban areas throughout Europe, the UK, North Africa and the Middle East

210. **Rufous owl** | *Ninox rufa* | Bird | Found in rainforests throughout northern Australia, Indonesia and Papua New Guinea

211. **Tawny fish-owl** | *Ketupa flavipes* | Bird | Found in forests and wetlands in parts of Asia and South-East Asia

212. **Spotted wood-owl** | *Strix seloputo* | Bird | Found in forests in South-East Asia

213. **Great horned owl** | *Bubo virginianus* | Bird | Found in a variety of habitats throughout North, Central and South America

214. **Powerful owl** | *Ninox strenua* | Bird | Found in forests, shrubland and wetlands of eastern Australia

215. **Great grey owl** | *Strix nebulosa* | Bird | Found in forests, shrubland, grassland and wetlands throughout northern North America, Europe and Asia

216. **Eurasian eagle-owl** | *Bubo bubo* | Bird | Found in forests, shrubland, grassland and caves throughout North Africa, Europe, the Middle East and Asia

About the artist

Tai Snaith is a Melbourne-based artist and writer. She has written and illustrated eight picture books to date, all published by Thames & Hudson. Tai has exhibited her paintings widely since graduating from the Victorian College of the Arts in 2002. She has created large site-specific visual installations for the Metro Creative program with Royal Botanic Gardens and The State Library of Victoria, which was shortlisted in the World Illustration Awards in London. Recently she created her first permanent public sculpture using twenty tonnes of natural stone for the Great Victorian Rail Trail. She has been awarded the Australia Council for the Arts Tokyo studio residency and numerous state and federal project grants. Tai's artwork is held in both private and public collections, including the NGA Works on Paper collection, Bayside and Banyule collections and Artbank.

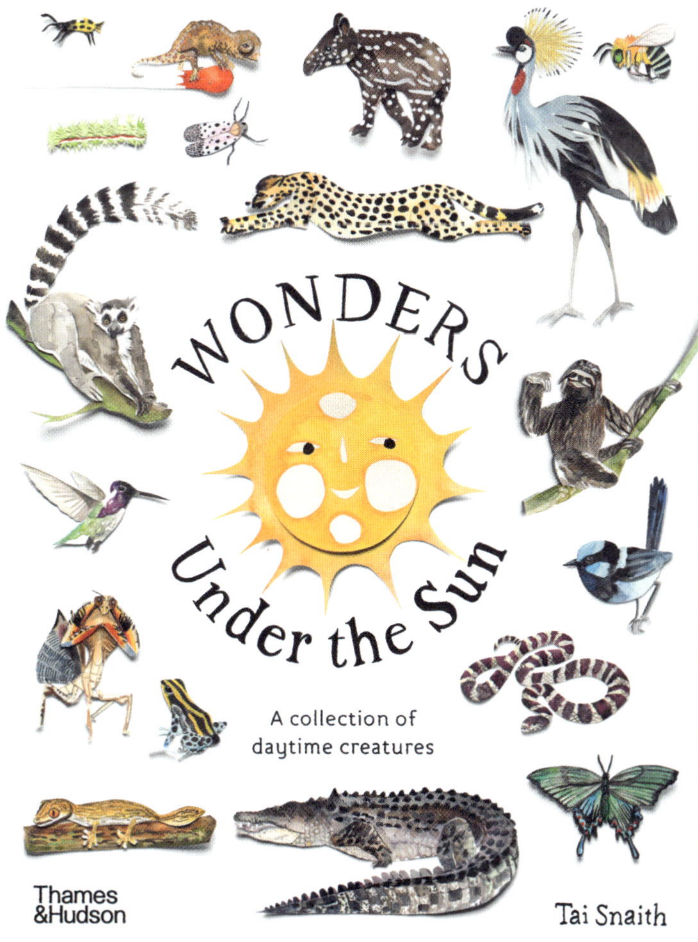

Thank you to Marta Cortada-McCorkell for all her research for this book.

First published in Australia in 2025 by Thames & Hudson Australia
Wurundjeri Country, 132A Gwynne Street, Cremorne, Victoria 3121

28 27 26 25 5 4 3 2 1

NATIONAL LIBRARY OF AUSTRALIA

A catalogue record for this book is available from the National Library of Australia

ISBN 978-1-760-76416-6

Design: Hope Lumsden-Barry
Editing: Nan McNab
Photography: Matthew Stanton
Author photo on p. 39: Marnie Goding

Printed and bound in China by RR Donnelley

FSC www.fsc.org MIX Paper | Supporting responsible forestry FSC® C144853

Thames & Hudson Australia wishes to acknowledge that Aboriginal and Torres Strait Islander peoples are the first storytellers of this nation and the Traditional Custodians of the land on which we live and work. We acknowledge their continuing culture and pay respect to Elders past and present.

thamesandhudson.com.au

Woodlands near streams

Shrublands and Savanna